**TO**

**FROM**

**DATE**

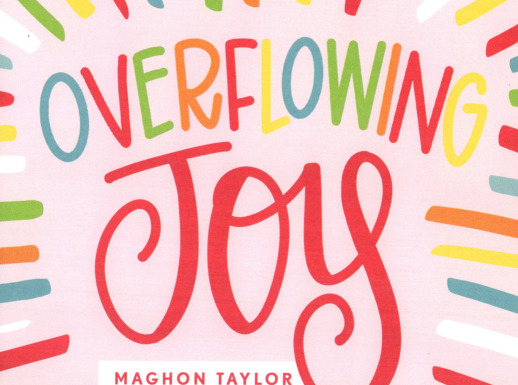

# OVERFLOWING JOY

**MAGHON TAYLOR**

An Inspirational Journal for

*celebrating*

Every Day

DaySpring

LIVE YOUR FAITH

_____
_____
_____
_____
_____
_____
_____
_____
_____
_____
_____
_____
_____
_____
_____
_____
_____
_____
_____
_____
_____
_____
_____
_____
_____
_____
_____

Absolutely nothing can get between us and God's love.

**ROMANS 8:39 THE MESSAGE**

_____

_____

_____

_____

_____

_____

_____

_____

_____

_____

_____

_____

_____

_____

_____

_____

_____

_____

_____

_____

_____

_____

_____

_____

_____

He has planted eternity in the human heart.

ECCLESIASTES 3:11 NLT

_____
_____
_____
_____
_____
_____
_____
_____
_____
_____
_____
_____
_____
_____
_____
_____
_____
_____
_____
_____
_____
_____
_____

**He chose us...that we would be holy and blameless before Him.**

EPHESIANS 1:4 NASB

_____

_____

_____

_____

_____

_____

_____

_____

_____

_____

_____

_____

_____

_____

_____

_____

_____

_____

_____

_____

_____

_____

_____

_____

_____

_____

God has chosen you and made you His holy people. He loves you.

**COLOSSIANS 3:12 ICB**

# Rejoice

This is the day the Lord has made;

let's rejoice and be glad in it.

PSALM 118:24 CSB

_____

_____

_____

_____

_____

_____

_____

_____

_____

_____

_____

_____

_____

_____

_____

_____

_____

_____

_____

_____

_____

_____

_____

He will be with you;

He will not leave you or abandon you.

**DEUTERONOMY 31:8 CSB**

_____

_____

_____

_____

_____

_____

_____

_____

_____

_____

_____

_____

_____

_____

_____

_____

_____

_____

_____

_____

_____

_____

_____

_____

_____

The LORD will fight for you,
and you have only to be silent.

EXODUS 14:14 ESV

By giving Himself completely at the Cross, actually dying for you,
Christ brought you over to God's side and put your lives together,
whole and holy in His presence.

COLOSSIANS 1:22 THE MESSAGE

# Remember

_____
_____
_____
_____
_____
_____
_____
_____
_____
_____
_____
_____
_____
_____
_____
_____
_____
_____
_____
_____
_____
_____
_____
_____
_____
_____
_____

Remember that the Lord your God is the only God and that He is faithful.
He will keep His covenant and show His constant love to
a thousand generations of those who love Him and obey His commands.

**DEUTERONOMY 7:9 GNT**

He has created us anew in Christ Jesus,
so we can do the good things He planned for us.

EPHESIANS 2:10 NLT

The Lord your God is with you wherever you go.

JOSHUA 1:9 CSB

You turned my lament into dancing.

PSALM 30:11 CSB

# Faith

You are saved by grace through faith...it is God's gift.

EPHESIANS 2:8 CSB

_____

_____

_____

_____

_____

_____

_____

_____

_____

_____

_____

_____

_____

_____

_____

_____

_____

_____

_____

_____

_____

_____

_____

I will give you a new heart and put a new spirit within you.

**EZEKIEL 36:26 CSB**

He Himself has said,
"I will never leave you or abandon you."

HEBREWS 13:5 CSB

_____

_____

_____

_____

_____

_____

_____

_____

_____

_____

_____

_____

_____

_____

_____

_____

_____

_____

_____

_____

_____

_____

_____

_____

A clean slate and a fresh start—
comes from God by way of Jesus Christ.

**I CORINTHIANS 1:30 THE MESSAGE**

# Hope

We have this hope as an anchor
for the soul, firm and secure.

HEBREWS 6:19 NIV

_____

_____

_____

_____

_____

_____

_____

_____

_____

_____

_____

_____

_____

_____

_____

_____

_____

_____

_____

_____

_____

_____

He will not let you be tempted beyond your ability.

**I CORINTHIANS 10:13 ESV**

_____
_____
_____
_____
_____
_____
_____
_____
_____
_____
_____
_____
_____
_____
_____
_____
_____
_____
_____
_____
_____
_____
_____
_____
_____

He cares about you.

I PETER 5:7 NLT

_____

_____

_____

_____

_____

_____

_____

_____

_____

_____

_____

_____

_____

_____

_____

_____

_____

_____

_____

_____

_____

_____

_____

_____

_____

He hears us.

**I JOHN 5:14 NASB**

# strong

_____

_____

_____

_____

_____

_____

_____

_____

_____

_____

_____

_____

_____

_____

_____

_____

_____

_____

_____

_____

_____

_____

_____

_____

_____

_____

He will keep you strong to the end so that you will be free
from all blame on the day when our Lord Jesus Christ returns.

I CORINTHIANS 1:8 NLT

_____

_____

_____

_____

_____

_____

_____

_____

_____

_____

_____

_____

_____

_____

_____

_____

_____

_____

_____

_____

_____

_____

_____

I will forgive their sin and will heal their land.

**II CHRONICLES 7:14 NIV**

He comforts us in all our troubles so that we can comfort others.

II CORINTHIANS 1:4 NLT

_____

_____

_____

_____

_____

_____

_____

_____

_____

_____

_____

_____

_____

_____

_____

_____

_____

_____

_____

_____

_____

_____

_____

Our inner person is being renewed day by day.

**II CORINTHIANS 4:16 CSB**

# creation

If anyone is in Christ, he is a new creation.

II CORINTHIANS 5:17 CSB

_____

_____

_____

_____

_____

_____

_____

_____

_____

_____

_____

_____

_____

_____

_____

_____

_____

_____

_____

_____

_____

_____

_____

_____

_____

Be strong;
don't give up, for your work has a reward.

**II CHRONICLES 15:7 CSB**

His divine power has given us everything required for life.

_____
_____
_____
_____
_____
_____
_____
_____
_____
_____
_____
_____
_____
_____
_____
_____
_____
_____
_____
_____
_____
_____
_____
_____
_____

He will strengthen you and protect you.

**II THESSALONIANS 3:3 NIV**

# Fearless

_____

_____

_____

_____

_____

_____

_____

_____

_____

_____

_____

_____

_____

_____

_____

_____

_____

_____

_____

_____

_____

_____

_____

_____

God has not given us a spirit of fear,
but one of power, love, and sound judgment.

II TIMOTHY 1:7 CSB

I will strengthen you, I will help you,
I will uphold you with my righteous right hand.

**ISAIAH 41:10 ESV**

Do not fear; I will help you.

_____

_____

_____

_____

_____

_____

_____

_____

_____

_____

_____

_____

_____

_____

_____

_____

_____

_____

_____

_____

_____

_____

_____

He gives power to the weak and strength to the powerless.

**ISAIAH 40:29 NLT**

# Wait

_____

_____

_____

_____

_____

_____

_____

_____

_____

_____

_____

_____

_____

_____

_____

_____

_____

_____

_____

_____

_____

_____

_____

_____

Those who wait for the Lord will gain new strength;
they will mount up with wings like eagles, they will run and not get tired,
they will walk and not become weary.

**ISAIAH 40:31 NASB**

A stronghold for the poor...
a refuge from storms and a shade from heat.

I will be with you...

When you walk through the fire, you will not be scorched.

ISAIAH 43:2 CSB

I made you, and I will care for you.
I will carry you along and save you.

ISAIAH 46:4 NLT

# Blessing

_____

_____

_____

_____

_____

_____

_____

_____

_____

_____

_____

_____

_____

_____

_____

_____

_____

_____

_____

_____

_____

_____

_____

_____

My faithful love for you will remain.
My covenant of blessing will never be broken.

ISAIAH 54:10 NLT

_____

_____

_____

_____

_____

_____

_____

_____

_____

_____

_____

_____

_____

_____

_____

_____

_____

_____

_____

_____

_____

_____

No weapon turned against you will succeed.

**ISAIAH 54:17 NLT**

_____

_____

_____

_____

_____

_____

_____

_____

_____

_____

_____

_____

_____

_____

_____

_____

_____

_____

_____

_____

_____

_____

_____

_____

I will be your God throughout your lifetime—
until your hair is white with age.

ISAIAH 46:4 NLT

_____
_____
_____
_____
_____
_____
_____
_____
_____
_____
_____
_____
_____
_____
_____
_____
_____
_____
_____
_____
_____
_____
_____
_____
_____

Though your sins are scarlet,
they will be as white as snow.

ISAIAH 1:18 CSB

# Forgiven

_____

_____

_____

_____

_____

_____

_____

_____

_____

_____

_____

_____

_____

_____

_____

_____

_____

_____

_____

_____

_____

_____

He...will forgive us our sins and purify us.

I JOHN 1:9 NIV

The Lord will continually guide you.

He never changes or casts a shifting shadow.

JAMES 1:17 NLT

_____
_____
_____
_____
_____
_____
_____
_____
_____
_____
_____
_____
_____
_____
_____
_____
_____
_____
_____
_____
_____
_____
_____
_____

Draw near to God,
and He will draw near to you.

JAMES 4:8 CSB

# Wise

Now if any of you lacks wisdom,
he should ask God...and it will be given to him.

JAMES 1:5 CSB

Humble yourselves before the Lord,
and He will lift you up.

**JAMES 4:10 NIV**

I will give you rain at the right time...
and the trees of the field will bear their fruit.

LEVITICUS 26:4 CSB

For nothing will be impossible with God.

LUKE 1:37 ESV

# future

I have it all planned out—plans to take care of you,
not abandon you, plans to give you the future you hope for.

Your Father knows the things you need before you ask Him.

MATTHEW 6:8 ICB

_____

_____

_____

_____

_____

_____

_____

_____

_____

_____

_____

_____

_____

_____

_____

_____

_____

_____

_____

_____

_____

_____

_____

Continue to ask, and God will give to you.
Continue to search, and you will find.
Continue to knock, and the door will open for you.

**MATTHEW 7:7 ICB**

_____
_____
_____
_____
_____
_____
_____
_____
_____
_____
_____
_____
_____
_____
_____
_____
_____
_____
_____
_____
_____
_____
_____
_____
_____

Give, and it will be given to you.

**LUKE 6:38 NIV**

# patience

_____
_____
_____
_____

_____
_____
_____
_____
_____
_____
_____
_____
_____
_____
_____
_____
_____
_____
_____
_____
_____
_____
_____
_____
_____
_____
_____
_____
_____
_____
_____
_____

_____

_____

_____

_____

_____

_____

_____

_____

_____

_____

_____

_____

_____

_____

_____

_____

_____

_____

_____

_____

_____

_____

_____

The Lord is good to those who wait for Him,

to the person who seeks Him.

**LAMENTATIONS 3:25 NASB**

_____

_____

_____

_____

_____

_____

_____

_____

_____

_____

_____

_____

_____

_____

_____

_____

_____

_____

_____

_____

_____

_____

_____

Call to Me and I will answer.

**JEREMIAH 33:3 NIV**

_____

_____

_____

_____

_____

_____

_____

_____

_____

_____

_____

_____

_____

_____

_____

_____

_____

_____

_____

_____

_____

_____

_____

_____

Those who drink the water I give will never be thirsty again.

JOHN 4:14 NLT

_____

_____

_____

_____

_____

_____

_____

_____

_____

_____

_____

_____

_____

_____

_____

_____

_____

_____

_____

_____

_____

_____

_____

I am the living bread....
Whoever eats this bread will live forever.

**JOHN 6:51 NIV**

# Believe

Anyone who believes in Me will live, even after dying.

I will send you the Helper from the Father.
He is the Spirit of truth who comes from the Father.

**JOHN 15:26 ICB**

Remain in Me, and I will remain in you.

JOHN 15:4 NLT

When the Spirit of truth comes,
He will guide you into all truth.

JOHN 16:13 NLT

# Joys

_____

_____

_____

_____

_____

_____

_____

_____

_____

_____

_____

_____

_____

_____

_____

_____

_____

_____

_____

_____

_____

_____

_____

_____

God, who...will bring you with great joy
into His glorious presence without a single fault.

JUDE 1:24 NLT

_____

_____

_____

_____

_____

_____

_____

_____

_____

_____

_____

_____

_____

_____

_____

_____

_____

_____

_____

_____

_____

_____

_____

_____

His mercies never end.

They are new every morning.

**LAMENTATIONS 3:22–23 CSB**

_____

_____

_____

_____

_____

_____

_____

_____

_____

_____

_____

_____

_____

_____

_____

_____

_____

_____

_____

_____

_____

_____

_____

_____

You're blessed when you're at the end of your rope.
With less of you there is more of God.

**MATTHEW 5:3 THE MESSAGE**

_____

_____

_____

_____

_____

_____

_____

_____

_____

_____

_____

_____

_____

_____

_____

_____

_____

_____

_____

_____

_____

_____

_____

Come to me,
all who labor and are heavy laden,
and I will give you rest.

**MATTHEW 11:28 ESV**

# Healed

I will give you back your health and heal your wounds.

JEREMIAH 30:17 NLT

_____

_____

_____

_____

_____

_____

_____

_____

_____

_____

_____

_____

_____

_____

_____

_____

_____

_____

_____

_____

_____

_____

_____

God's peace will keep your hearts and minds in Christ Jesus.

**PHILIPPIANS 4:7 ICB**

_____

_____

_____

_____

_____

_____

_____

_____

_____

_____

_____

_____

_____

_____

_____

_____

_____

_____

_____

_____

_____

_____

_____

I can do all things through Christ because He gives me strength.

**PHILIPPIANS 4:13 ICB**

_____

_____

_____

_____

_____

_____

_____

_____

_____

_____

_____

_____

_____

_____

_____

_____

_____

_____

_____

_____

_____

_____

God will meet all your needs.

PHILIPPIANS 4:19 NIV

# prayer

_____

_____

_____

_____

_____

_____

_____

_____

_____

_____

_____

_____

_____

_____

_____

_____

_____

_____

_____

_____

_____

_____

_____

_____

Don't fret or worry.

Instead of worrying, pray.

**PHILIPPIANS 4:6 THE MESSAGE**

_____

_____

_____

_____

_____

_____

_____

_____

_____

_____

_____

_____

_____

_____

_____

_____

_____

_____

_____

_____

_____

_____

_____

_____

The Lord is good, a stronghold in the day of trouble.

**NAHUM 1:7 ESV**

He will make your paths straight.

PROVERBS 3:6 CSB

He is a shield to those who take refuge in Him.

# Grace

_____

_____

_____

_____

_____

_____

_____

_____

_____

_____

_____

_____

_____

_____

_____

_____

_____

_____

_____

_____

_____

_____

_____

_____

The God of all grace...

will himself restore, confirm, strengthen, and establish you.

**I PETER 5:10 ESV**

He lets me lie down in green pastures;

He leads me beside quiet waters.

**PSALM 23:2 CSB**

_____

_____

_____

_____

_____

_____

_____

_____

_____

_____

_____

_____

_____

_____

_____

_____

_____

_____

_____

_____

_____

_____

He renews my life;

He leads me along the right paths for His name's sake.

**PSALM 23:3 CSB**

_____

_____

_____

_____

_____

_____

_____

_____

_____

_____

_____

_____

_____

_____

_____

_____

_____

_____

_____

_____

_____

_____

_____

_____

The Lord gives His people strength;

the Lord blesses His people with peace.

**PSALM 29:11 CSB**

# filled

_____
_____
_____
_____
_____
_____
_____
_____
_____
_____
_____
_____
_____
_____
_____
_____
_____
_____
_____
_____
_____
_____
_____
_____
_____
_____
_____
_____
_____

You will fill me with joy in Your presence.

PSALM 16:11 NIV

He will sustain you;
He will never allow the righteous to be shaken.

**PSALM 55:22 NASB**

_____
_____
_____
_____
_____
_____
_____
_____
_____
_____
_____
_____
_____
_____
_____
_____
_____
_____
_____
_____
_____
_____
_____
_____
_____
_____

Day after day He bears our burdens.

**PSALM 68:19 CSB**

_____

_____

_____

_____

_____

_____

_____

_____

_____

_____

_____

_____

_____

_____

_____

_____

_____

_____

_____

_____

_____

_____

_____

_____

_____

But You, Lord, are a shield around me, my glory,
and the One who lifts up my head.

**PSALM 3:3 CSB**

# peace

_____
_____
_____
_____
_____
_____
_____
_____
_____
_____
_____
_____
_____
_____
_____
_____
_____
_____
_____
_____
_____
_____

Peace I leave with you.
My peace I give to you.

**JOHN 14:27 CSB**

_____

_____

_____

_____

_____

_____

_____

_____

_____

_____

_____

_____

_____

_____

_____

_____

_____

_____

_____

_____

_____

_____

_____

You are a hiding place for me;

you preserve me from trouble.

**PSALM 32:7 ESV**

The Lord is near the brokenhearted;
He saves those crushed in spirit.

PSALM 34:18 CSB

You protect people as a bird protects her young under her wings.

# Heart

Take delight in the Lord,
and He will give you your heart's desires.

PSALM 37:4 CSB

_____

_____

_____

_____

_____

_____

_____

_____

_____

_____

_____

_____

_____

_____

_____

_____

_____

_____

_____

_____

_____

_____

The Lord grants favor and honor;
He does not withhold the good from those who live with integrity.

**PSALM 84:11 CSB**

_____

_____

_____

_____

_____

_____

_____

_____

_____

_____

_____

_____

_____

_____

_____

_____

_____

_____

_____

_____

_____

_____

_____

_____

He will give His angels orders...

to protect you in all your ways.

**PSALM 91:11 CSB**

_____

_____

_____

_____

_____

_____

_____

_____

_____

_____

_____

_____

_____

_____

_____

_____

_____

_____

_____

_____

_____

_____

_____

_____

_____

He will rejoice over you with gladness...

He will delight in you with singing.

**ZEPHANIAH 3:17 CSB**

# Faithful

His faithful love endures forever.

He satisfies you with good things;

your youth is renewed like the eagle.

**PSALM 103:5 CSB**

The Lord has compassion on those who fear Him.

PSALM 103:13 CSB

_____

_____

_____

_____

_____

_____

_____

_____

_____

_____

_____

_____

_____

_____

_____

_____

_____

_____

_____

_____

_____

_____

He will not allow your foot to slip;
He who keeps you will not slumber.

**PSALM 121:3 NASB**

# Light

_____

_____

_____

_____

_____

_____

_____

_____

_____

_____

_____

_____

_____

_____

_____

_____

_____

_____

_____

_____

_____

_____

_____

_____

_____

If you follow Me, you won't have to walk in darkness,
because you will have the light that leads to life.

**JOHN 8:12 NLT**

The Son of Man came to find and restore the lost.